handwritten inscription: Thanks for this,

handwritten inscription: ... is this book

MY

FACES

OF

DEATH

A Deadly Memoir
John Alan Schwartz

signature: John Alan Schwartz

The truth behind the making
of the cult film banned in 47 countries

ANCHORAGE PRESS
LOS ANGELES 2014

ISBN: 978-1500131876

Cover Art: Paul Mcvay and Lisa Vasquez

Anchorage Press
245 South Serrano Avenue
Suit 313
LA CA 90004

Printed in the United States of America

"For the living… and for the dying."
– Dr. Francis B. Gross,
Pathologist, FACES OF DEATH

INTRODUCTION

We live in a world that is manipulated by the media.
I should know. 35 years ago I created FACES OF DEATH, voted
the 27th most controversial film of all time. Of course, what I really
did was fool people around the world. At its peak the movie was
banned in 47 countries. To date the film has grossed over 60 million
dollars.

What made FACES OF DEATH so controversial was that
people couldn't tell the difference between fact and fiction. We
took real life footage and combined it with recreated footage so that
we were fabricating reality before it became a trend decades later.
FACES OF DEATH never seems to lose its popularity generation
after generation. I'm still asked to do interviews, nationally and
internationally—at least in countries that have lifted the ban!

It takes a communal effort to make a film and that was the
case with FACES OF DEATH. With our small, experienced crew
and special effects team, we broke boundary after boundary, until,
as things got truly bizarre, we grew convinced there was a strange
force surrounding us. A lot of frightening things happened, but that
never stopped us. Given artistic freedom we kept plunging forward,
seeing how extreme and outrageous we could be and how far we
were willing to go into the darkest recesses of death.

In this book I will reveal for the first time the true stories behind the making of FACES OF DEATH, the layers of death we explored, and what we were forced to confront. This was one project that touched each of our souls.

I remember when we screened the film before an audience of 500 people at 20th Century Fox. As the end credits rolled, there was complete silence. Everyone was blown away. At the time I was dating a girl whose father was a physician. He came up to me and said this was the most intense and ground breaking exploration of death he had ever seen.

There were actually four FACES OF DEATH films, plus a fact or fiction supplement. I like the first FACES OF DEATH the most. There is an innocence and insanity that gives the movie a unique tone. Our original budget for FACES OF DEATH was $450,000.00 and we came in under budget!

Oftentimes people ask: how do you create a cult classic? The answer is easy, because you can't. You need luck and not being afraid to go all the way. And I do mean all the way. When you do that maybe you'll click with something everyone shares but hasn't been able to face. In the end, that's what FACES OF DEATH was all about—shining light on the one thing we all have to face.

These days reality television rules the medium. Everyone is looking for their fifteen minutes of fame. Most of the shows have become homogenized and repetitious. People often ask me what the next level of reality television might be. Perhaps it will be a show that tracks the demise and destruction of humanity. After all, why couldn't a terrorist group armed with a dirty bomb shoot their own reality show before they blow up the world? I'm sure it would get high ratings, assuming there was an audience alive to watch!

Now from my place on the beach in Southern California, it's finally time to tell my story of how we made FACES OF DEATH; what happened to us along the way, the fight between light and dark, and how in the end most of us, but not all, managed to survive.

CHAPTER 1: THE BEGINNING

I guess I should tell you a little about myself so you can know how my mind works.

I was born in 1952 in a town just north of New York City. I remember little about my early upbringing. I knew for sure that our house seemed haunted. It was an old house, a small plantation design with three pillars on the outside, and it was always creaking and shaking slightly, as if invisible hands were playing with our souls.

There was an attic into which we were never permitted to go. My father, who was a salesman, threatened grave punishment if we ventured into the attic. My brother Jim, four years older and a later collaborator on the fourth FACES OF DEATH film, could not contain his desire to see what the attic contained.

One day, when my mother was out and my dad at work, we went up to the attic. My brother found the attic door key in a pair of my father's shoes. I couldn't believe we were doing it.

I was a good boy. I tried to do the right thing. I felt like I was desecrating a sacred trust, once when broken, could never be put back together. Nevertheless, the lure of the forbidden was too powerful.

The attic door swung open with a loud series of creaks. It was dark. A slanted ceiling ran from corner to corner. The room itself was small; only a bit of light passed through an oblong of a window on the far side. There was a sweet, decaying smell in the air. At first, the room seemed to be empty. Then, as our eyes became acclimated, we made out a solitary item in the middle of the room, it appeared to be a table or desk or some other piece of furniture.

I begged my brother to get out. He told me to shut up. He found a string hanging from a light bulb. He yanked the string and a small, twenty-five watt bulb went on, casting a wan light. It wasn't a desk or a table in that room. Not anything of the sort.

It was a coffin. A rough wood coffin, unpainted, and unvarnished. The letters K C had been carved into a center panel. The coffin lid didn't seem to be nailed down, merely secured by a clasp on the side.

Neither of us could speak. Who was in the coffin? Was there somebody in it? And what was a coffin doing in our house?

Though our curiosity drove us crazy, there was no way we were going to open that coffin. I imagined unspeakable demons encased in that box.

My brother pulled the light string, the room went dark and we backed out. I could barely breathe. My brother locked the door and replaced the key in my father's shoe. He made me promise never to tell my dad what we had done. I wasn't good at keeping secrets, but was afraid if I told my dad what we had done I would wind up in the coffin.

Little did I know how right I was.

CHAPTER 2: EARLY CHILDHOOD

I look back all the time at my childhood to see if there were defining moments. Events that prepared me for my descent into death and madness and the first three FACES Of DEATH films.

I came up against a brick wall. Oh, sure, there was that coffin. Later, when my brother and I were especially bad, my father would drag one of us up to the attic, kicking and screaming, and put us in the coffin. The amount of time we were in the coffin depended on what we did wrong. Once, my father found me inserting Vaseline laden q-tips into our pet dog's anus and I went into the coffin for three hours. When I came out, I was practically crazy. I was hallucinating. I couldn't stop crying. You have no idea what it's like to be confined in a coffin, unable to breathe or move, wondering if you'd ever get out. All the dog did was look at me with loving eyes. I could hardly tell my dad the dog enjoyed the experience.

Mostly I remained alone with my thoughts. My parents didn't want much to do with me and neither did my brother. I fantasized all the time. I thought of foreign lands and places where spirits ruled. I wasn't thrilled with humans in general. Although I had friends in school, I felt like a loner.

I engaged in sports and was a good athlete. My grades were okay. I seemed normal. On the surface it was cool. But I was like the Los Angeles landscape, which to all appearances is normal but sits on a fault line, ready to blow at any time. Something was happening inside me.

One day, I saw a spider web in our back yard. A huge spider was lurking in the corner, waiting for its prey. A fly flew into the web. It wriggled in a useless attempt to get out. The spider just sat there. When the fly's movement slowed, the spider crawled up the web toward the fly. It remained a short distance from the fly. In the next moment, the spider lunged and clasped the little fly head it its mandible. The fly had no chance. The spider sucked the life out of the fly while it was still alive.

It was a horrible death. At first, I pitied the poor fly. I thought what a misfortune, to stumble into that web. The fly was just having a normal day, enjoying its fly life. Then it all became hell for him.
I thought of the fact that all animals were part of the food chain. Except for humans. We were at the top. We didn't have to worry about being hunted and being eaten. What great luck that, unlike the fly, we couldn't stumble into a web and have the life sucked out of us.

Then I thought of all the accidents that befall humans. And all the diseases that, like the spider web, ensnare humans and suck the life out of them.

A thought came to me, one that I would be obsessed by for most of my life. What if there was something above us? What if we were part of the food chain, except that the power was one we could not see? What if this force was revealed after we passed from this life? What if there was some huge power orchestrating our demise, like what the spider was doing to the fly?

I guess my thinking wasn't original. It's what religions had been talking about for thousands of years. For me, it opened up the real possibility that there was truly something other than this obvious life on earth. Something to be explored and explained, if possible. When it comes down to it, my making of the FACES OF DEATH movies many years later was my attempt to do just that.

CHAPTER 3: THE LURE OF THE HORRIBLE

I have always been attracted to the horrible. Even these days, what attracts me in movies is violence honestly depicted. I despise filmmakers who phony up violence or cut it unrealistically. How can I have an appreciation for the gruesome unless it mimics the blood-spurting reality of life?

I used to get mad at people who slowed traffic just to stare at a bad accident, but now I enjoy looking at such accidents. So how can I blame them?

When some maniac goes crazy and shoots up a school or factory or airbase, I read about it with great interest. It's not that I don't pity the victims. Of course I do. The violence, the insanity, the proximity of death is what attracts me and always has.

When I was about nine, I went out into the woods with some friends. We were hiking when we came upon three older, tough high school boys.

They held us against our will for the better part of the afternoon. They engaged in escalating acts of violence. At first, they pushed us around. Then they slapped and threatened to kill us. They had fireworks. They made me hold a cherry bomb and lit it. I threw it away just before it would have blown off my hand. They laughed and one punched me in the mouth. Blood was pouring out of my face. To this day I have a scar just over the right side of my upper lip.

One of them produced a rope and threw it over a tree branch. They made a noose in the bottom of the rope. They asked which of us was a Jew. We all were, but at that moment none of us felt very religious.

They picked my friend Mark. They made him stand on a milk crate. He was crying. A stream of urine flowed from beneath his pants. They put the noose around his neck. He begged them to stop.

It was horrible but there was a part of me that was excited by the hanging. I was wondering what Mark would look like, thrashing about on that rope as his life went out of him. Sort of what happened to the fly in the spider web.

One of the guys kicked the milk crate away. Mark dangled for a couple of seconds. His face was so red I thought it would burst. Then the rope snapped and Mark tumbled to the ground. To this day I don't know if they would have killed him.

The thugs beat us for a while longer and eventually got bored. They told us if we told anyone about this they would kill us. I believed them. When I got home, it was way past dinnertime. I told my parents I was playing a big game of basketball. They wondered why my mouth was bleeding. I told them it happened while I was going up for a rebound.

Tragedies compel human beings. Perhaps it is our way of expressing gratitude that it is not us. Perhaps because tragedies herald death we are compelled to watch them, as if knowledge of our eventual demise will be revealed.

People want to feel. Be it the bright side of love or compassion or connection with darkness of that which is shocking or revolting, humans crave that which jars them from the ordinary and offers connection to something greater. That which is greater exists in the huge collective unconscious, that which occurs before and after us, and is limitless and incomprehensible.

Nothing is more incomprehensible than death. Nothing. It is the great mystery. The wheel of fate spins and spins. When it lands on our space, it is over for us. We never know when it will be. Perhaps we believe if it happens to somebody else, the odds of us going on a bit longer get better.

Of course that is not true. The longer we are alive, the shorter our odds and it has nothing to do with what happens to anybody else.

For a long time I thought I was sick and twisted because I found violence and scenes of death compelling. It was very liberating to finally realize that most people, especially young men, felt the same way.

I was later to discover the commercial possibilities inherent in such a widespread appreciation during my making of FACES OF DEATH.

CHAPTER 4: CHILDHOOD CONTINUES

Because I was ignored by my family, I spent lots of time in my mind and in my imagination. Where others had bonds with the living, my associations were with the spirits that roamed in my thoughts. There was no difference between these entities and the real humans who moved about me.

Later in life, when I took LSD, I had tangible proof the images in one's mind could be just as real as evidence provided by the senses, and that as a youth I had not been "crazy." My mind was the soil in which the idea for the study of death would take root.

I began to notice what I called "little deaths" in life. The disappointment that a classmate felt when he or she was rejected by another classmate. The horrified expression on a fellow student's face before or during an exam. These were little abysses that we looked into every day, little deaths that foreshadowed the ultimate mystery.

Even more compelling was what occurred when a student was reprimanded in front of the class. You could see, in the student's embarrassment, a slight cessation of life, a withdrawal from the living. I would see it in my dog, when she would become sick, and slink into a corner until she felt better. Or, if she did not, prepare herself for the great mystery from that place of withdrawal.

As with the thugs who tortured me that day in the woods,

I saw evidence of more literal little deaths all the time. One day during recess, one of the bullies beat up a student foolish enough to stand up for himself. The bully punched the kid to the ground and then delivered drop kick after drop kick to the prostrate kid. It was a "little death" vividly told.

Later, in the classroom, I couldn't get the image out of my head. Was it only that which destroyed that unleashed the mystery of the beyond? As I was reflecting on this, the social studies teacher was reviling the incident, talking about the horror of violence and the need to kill one another with kindness.

I sat up with a jolt. Kill one another with kindness. Now there was a novel idea. I knew violence, and mayhem had the ability to transform and fascinate. Could one kill with kindness? Could one die from pleasure? And if so, would the fear of death be reduced or made more easily accepted?

The idea remained a mystery until several years later during my first experience with sexual intercourse. The girl was older than I and the experience was all I had dreamed. The pleasure was intense. Of course, like any young man I had no control and ejaculated prematurely.

Just before I came, I felt the mounting rush of incipient orgasm. I felt like I was rushing through a tunnel towards a happy death. When I came, I lost consciousness for a moment. For that brief instant, I had been killed with pleasure, with kindness. Sex, I was to learn, like violence, can help us unravel the mystery of death. It is why, like violence, it sells so well.

CHAPTER 5: GESTATION

When I was fifteen, my parents sent me off to boarding school. I was glad to be away from the coffin, in which I had spent too many hours.

The school was in upstate New York. Unlike the public school system, in which I had been ignored because of my brooding, quiet nature, I was regarded by my pseudo-intellectual private school buddies as being deep and profound. The fact that I read philosophy endlessly, cemented my reputation. In my junior year, although I ran a campaign in which my slogan was "Sartre wouldn't vote," I was elected president of my class in a landslide.

The less I wanted attention, the more I seemed to get it. Several of the teachers befriended me. One day, in her house, my female ethics instructor asked if she could give me a blow job. At first I was weirded out. Although she was pretty, she was old enough to be my mom. I was also concerned this involvement could affect my grades.

She gave me a great blow job. Over time we had intercourse, too. The problem was that she began to have feelings for me. She would tell me she loved me and wait for me to say I loved her back. I felt like I had to say it to make sure she gave me good grades.

She began to talk about letting people know about our affair. I was freaked out. I thought about what my parents would think. I told the teacher she would get in a lot of trouble if she people found out about us.

Although I craved the sex, I began to hate myself for what we were doing. As the year went on and she insisted on my not wearing protection so she could get pregnant and have our baby I hated myself more and more. I saw that if I continued like that I might kill myself.

I wondered about suicide. I wondered if the taking of one's own life was a brave or cowardly act. When a Tibetan monk immolated himself in protest of war, was that bravery or cowardice? When a schizophrenic man jumped onto a railroad track on his mother's birthday in an attempt to communicate or apologize to her, was that an act of bravery or cowardice?

I did not know. What I did know was that I was moving perilously close to a precipice. None of my classmates knew what was going on. I would preside at school meetings in a state of complete withdrawal, which they took for inner genius.

One night I had a revelation. It was a message from God. I have had many messages from God since. You have, too. The key is that when they are rendered, to take heed. You can tell a message is from God because it feels so right. It is how Moses felt when he got the commandments.

I was going up an escalator in a department store. This voice, out of nowhere said, "It is the ultimate sacrilege to take your own life. Never take your own life." It boomed within me and filled my soul.

This became gospel for me. The next day I told the teacher that what transpired between us was over. She cried and begged me to fuck her. I told her if she uttered that desire again, I would treat her to a glimpse of the great mystery.

Yes, I told her I would kill her. And I was prepared to do it, too. Although I believed that taking my own life was sacrilege, it was not, under some circumstances, a sacrilege to take another person's life.

Some serial killers have said as much

John Wayne Gacy once said that under the right circumstances, killing clears the sinuses better than hot sauce.

CHAPTER 6: THE GERM OF AN IDEA

While at boarding school I got involved in acting. I wasn't really into it. I was attracted to the arts. I had always loved live theater and the movies. Since my school didn't have film classes, drama was the next best thing.

I got a couple of lead roles. Although people said I was a good actor, I always felt I was merely a vessel for the writer's words. It always felt like I was "acting."

I loved being able to move an audience, to affect a change in them. To me that is the greatest thing about the arts. The act of witnessing something theatrical can temporarily alter a person's personality.

That change doesn't last very long, at least not usually. There are great moments in movie theaters when, like at the end of "Rocky," one is moved to tears by the hero overcoming incredible odds and seeing love created.

Then the viewer goes outside the movie theater and has a few beers and some pizza with the boys and the movie becomes a recollection and not something life altering.

I wanted to be part of something theatrical that would not only affect those seeing it in real time, but permanently alter the psychic DNA of the viewer.

This idea to create something iconoclastic bumped around

my head from time to time. Although I played the harmonica pretty well and saw music as a medium for great change, I never developed the interest or chops to persist in a musical career.

But movies, that was another matter. I loved movies. And I realized everybody else did, too. There is no greater escape than in a good movie.

The cinema experience is very tribal. One might ask why movie theaters are more popular today than ever. After all, everybody has a huge screen at home and you can get a first run movie seemingly weeks after it opens in movie theaters.

There is something about going into a huge, cavernous room with hundreds of strangers, surrounded by thunderous sounds, and flashing lights. It becomes a communal experience. The impact on one viewer is magnified by the simultaneous impact on hundreds of other viewers. The moans, screams, and cries of many are rendered more powerful in the individual viewer's soul.

I remember when I saw Lawrence of Arabia, one of the most beautiful movies ever made, and Peter O'Toole blows out a match and the scene cuts to the huge expanse of desert. The collective gasp in the audience created a memory within me that will never be erased.

I wanted to create moments like that for my fellow human beings, not prance around a stage "acting" like a character some clever writer had imagined.

Maybe I was secretly seeking a piece of immortality, something that would last after I passed through this vale of tears. Maybe I was just seeking to be part of something larger than myself.

CHAPTER 7: LOVE

After I broke off the affair with my ethics teacher, I began to obsess on sex. It was too bad I was at an all male school. If I was gay, I would have had a field day. I even thought about asking the ethics teacher to resume our relationship. Then I thought about how crazy she was, and about the "F" she had given me on my final exam, even though I knew I had done well. I knew I could never return to that dangerous place.

I guess what I got from boarding school was a love of learning. I began to appreciate the nuances of writers from Goethe to Hemingway to Hegel to Shakespeare.

During the summer of my junior year, I returned to Manhattan to work for my father at his textile firm. I lived in my parent's condo on the east side. I met a woman in her late 20's who worked at his office as a designer. I thought she was beautiful, and she was funny and nice, and she seemed to really like me.

We went out to dinner a couple of times and then one night after work, she invited me up to her apartment. When I got there the door was ajar. I called out "hello" and I heard a soft voice call out that she was in the bedroom. It was a small apartment, like most in NYC, and I went through a kitchen that contained a bathtub and a refrigerator and into the tiny bedroom.

I discovered she was naked under the sheets. She told me to

take my clothes off. I got in with her. It was in the bed of this woman where I discovered the essence of life. She taught me the joy of love and sex and it was uninhibited, grand, and luscious.

It ran its course, though, and although we were sad when I had to return for my senior year, we vowed to write and look forward to time together over the holidays.

The depth of sexual feeling is as great a mystery as death. It is the greatest single motivating force on this planet. The need to kill is only love subverted into hate. If more men had sex they would be less inclined to kill. There was a psychologist, Wilhelm Reich, who started to influence me. I read this book called "The Function Of The Orgasm" where Reich describes how the orgasm is the only thing that can relieve tension in the male. Without it, bad things can happen.

Back at school I fantasized about my NYC sweetheart. I dreamed about going to a coed college. There was no chance of my going to an all male school. In fact, I obsessed so much about sex that I thought about applying to all-women's schools. I heard a few of them, like Wellesley, were to start going coed. I thought that was a good idea, to be the first male in a formerly all women's school. I thought of how horny those juniors and seniors would have to be. And I was ready to take care of them all.

CHAPER 8: MARKING TIME

I went back for my senior year at boarding school obsessed with my New York City lady friend. I called every chance I could. After a month, she stopped returning my calls. After my nineteenth unreturned call, she picked up. She told me that my father insisted that she leave me alone. That it was better for me to concentrate on my school work and she on her designing.

I fell into a depression. I began to drink and smoke a lot of dope. My grand plans to alter the course of humanity through cinema were put on the back burner. I masturbated so much it's a miracle my penis didn't fall off.

It was Thanksgiving of that year that I think I killed someone. I was home for the holidays. Even though I was staying at my parents' house, I was boozing up a storm. The night after Thanksgiving, I went to a friend's house. Afterwards, while waiting for the subway, a young drunk guy nursing a quart of Olde English Ale began cursing at the top of his lungs. He pissed me off.

Even though he was a burly guy and scraggly I went over, picked up his bottle of booze, and smashed it on the subway platform. It broke into a thousand pieces sending the amber fluid spilling onto the tracks. Just then the train pulled into the station. I got on one car, he got on another.

Before the train had gotten a hundred yards out of the station, the drunk guy had positioned himself in between the cars and was banging on the my car window. I was surprised his hand didn't go through the glass.

Maybe it was because I was drunk or maybe the forces of the Universe had put me in a dark place. I ran over to the door, yanked it open and screamed at the guy. I frightened him so badly that he lurched backward and fell off the side of the car. I watched his head smash into a wall and saw him disappear beneath the train wheels.

He was gone in an instant. I went back inside the car. There were only two people on the car and both had their heads buried in their newspapers. Like any good New Yorkers, they wanted no extra problems in their lives.

I got off at the next stop. I walked the last forty blocks to my parents' house. The next day I watched every news show waiting to hear about a dead guy on the subway tracks. There was nothing.

It was strange but I didn't feel bad about what had happened. If the guy died, it was his time. That's all I thought. He didn't seem like such a great contributor to the human race. His loss would be mourned by few, if any. It wasn't like I had helped kill Jonas Salk or Albert Einstein.

I began to wonder if the incident had ever occurred. I was wondering what was real and what wasn't.

One thing that was for real was that I was thrown out of private school just before the end of the semester. I was the star basketball player and instead of going to the championship game I found myself getting hammered in a bar with the dean of admissions. He got canned and I was sent packing to finish the second semester being home-schooled by my folks.

At this point, I was in survival mode. All my lofty creative dreams were on hold. I was a loser, a kid just a stone's throw from the street.

CHAPTER 9: ANOTHER DEATH HAUNTS ME

Home schooling wasn't so bad. It was a lot easier than boarding school. My mother had received her Masters in Montessori training. This was the kind of philosophy that basically let kids do whatever interested them. So I read a lot of film books, and in between, satisfied my requirements to get into college. My SAT's were nothing to rave about. I wasn't going to go to an Ivy League School. Then again, I didn't want to. Just some place with a lot of babes.

My dad insisted I help pay for my room, board, and education. So I got a job driving a yellow taxi. I drove Friday, Saturday, and Sunday nights. I started at about 3 in the afternoon and finished up at about 3 in the morning. I became friends with many of the drivers. Most of them got behind the wheel high on something. I was one of the few who didn't. I was living at home and my grasp on that situation was tenuous to say the least.

It was while driving the cab that I had my next encounter with death.

It was late Saturday night. I was coming down 9th Avenue just south of Port Authority. You had to be careful who you picked up in that area. Lots of human cockroaches crawled out of Port Authority during the wee hours.

It was slow and my judgment was off. I picked up three young guys and the second they were in the back seat, I knew I had made a mistake. The smell of glue hung in the air. One carried a paper bag. I knew they had been sniffing. Their eyes were bloodshot. One of them told me to go to Sheepshead Bay in Brooklyn.

There was no way I was going to go there. The best case scenario would be that they wouldn't pay me. The worst case would that they would shoot me in the head. And all the places in between weren't pretty to contemplate, either.

I told them my grandmother was dying and I had to go the hospital. If I wasn't with dear Grams, I would never forgive myself. One of them said, "Fuck your grandmother." and insisted I go to Brooklyn.

Calmly, I told them no way could I do that. But I'd take them down to a diner on 21st Street and from there they could get another cab easily. One of them put the bag over his face and inhaled deeply. He then passed the bag to the other bozos.

We got to the diner. The tab was $2.80. I told them it was on the house. I turned around with a smile. As the first one was getting out of the cab, he spit in my face. The second one spit in my face, too. Huge gobs of fresh mucous ran down my nose. The third one hawked a loogie into my face as well.

As he was getting out of the cab, I floored it. He hung on as long as he could while running alongside the cab. I can still hear his screams. Then he fell and I heard a gruesome clunk as the door smashed into and crushed his skull. As I zoomed away, I saw him lying in the street.

I ran several red lights in an attempt to put distance between myself and the horror. Finally, after about twenty blocks, I permitted myself to pull over. My heart was racing.

I was mortified. I thought I really hurt the guy, maybe killed him. Why was death following me? And who would be next?

CHAPTER 10: JUST BEFORE COLLEGE

I was playing basketball one day down on 4th Street in Manhattan. They called the place Ego Park because there was always a crowd watching and the players drove themselves to new heights to show off their skills. Players would hurl themselves with abandon up and down the court risking life and limb to thrill the crowd and some inner part of themselves that felt immortal.

I thought about that. Young people think they're immortal. The idea of aging, sickness, and death is unimaginable. That is why so many young men volunteer for the Armed Services during time of war. They can't imagine they'll be the ones to have their arms or legs shot off. No, they are filled with the intrepid juice of life. Give young boys a gun and a dream of being a hero and they're sold. The charge of immortality in the young and the loss of joy among the old have fueled more wars than the quest for morality or goodness ever have.

It was in that light that I began to consider the subway incident and the cab experience. Here I had participated in the possible demise of two young men. I had helped end their lives and ushered them through the portal to a darkness they had only seen on TV and in the movies. Through them, I was being put in touch with something greater than myself. I was learning at a young age that there was a limit to this life.

I wondered why this was happening to me. I tried to

discuss this with my parents and they asked if I would like to see a psychologist. I went out with a woman a couple of times and she stopped seeing me, accusing me of being depressed. To me there was nothing wrong with inquiring about the nature of death. After all, without it life would have no meaning.

Although the news on TV de-sensitizes us to the importance of death and makes it seem commonplace, I became an avid newshound. The fear the news induced in others provided me with a sense of freedom. There was a way to transcend the fear of death and that was to experience it in life, not as a grim montage, but by embracing the moment. Everything I did had a new importance.

CHAPTER 11: COLLEGE

I had my choice of a few colleges. I decided to go to Emerson in Boston. I liked the city and it had an old world charm and modern relevance. The school was small and had an active arts department. Mostly I liked it because it was coed and had a campus teeming with nubile beauties After years of all male schools, I felt as if I had died and gone to heaven.

I wish I could say I nurtured the dream of being an artist and studied hard. Truth was that I did little else other than get high and get laid. I became good friends with my roommate, Joe, and cut a wide swath through the women at Emerson.

Although I thought I was through with acting, it still appealed to me, mainly because it was the easiest. I joined an otherwise all black acting troupe and had some minor roles in Pinter and Arthur Miller plays. Although I received kudos for my performances, I had no real passion for the craft.

In my sophomore year, I fell in love with a pretty young coed whose father was an ear, nose and throat doctor. I soon discovered he used cocaine in some of his treatments. Although my ear, nose and throat were fine, I administered the cocaine to myself. I enjoyed the buzz, but I was primarily a grass and Quaalude kind of guy.

Quaaludes were the greatest aphrodisiac imaginable. After I took a couple of those pills, the closest woman became a goddess and I was ready to ramble. My brother came to visit one day and brought a bagful. He passed them out to all my dorm mates and pretty soon we had the largest orgy in the history of Emerson.

After a day or two, I lost track of my brother. My roommate invited me out to a pub that had great fish and chips. I realized I hadn't eaten anything but Quaaludes for two or three days and so I braved a serious snowstorm in search of fried foods. After eating enough for an army, Joe and I trudged through the snow back to the dorm. It was coming down in sheets and there must have been a foot or more on the ground.

At some point, we noticed a stalled car being pushed out of the roadway by a lone individual. Joe and I decided to help. Lo and behold, there pushing the car was my brother. Somehow we had connected, mysteriously, in the middle of a snowstorm, on an anonymous street in Boston.

I loved my brother, but later that night he put my love to the test. After I fell asleep, not to waken for maybe a day or two, he fed Quaaludes to my beloved girlfriend and banged her all night. When I found out about it I was enraged, but after a Quaalude or two I was filled with love for the Universe, my brother included.

My brother would re-enter my life many times over the years. After surviving the hell of my household, he and I were like soldiers who survive a war in the foxholes and were inextricably bonded.

CHAPTER 12: MORE COLLEGE

I never thought I could grow tired of getting high and having sex. But by the end of my freshman year I was. Some kernel of creativity was growing within me that demanded to be nurtured. And, clearly, Emerson wasn't doing it.

I increasingly felt bored with acting. I think an actor, or anybody, must be driven to be successful. I didn't have that drive. As high as I was, it was a miracle I could even enunciate my lines. Once, in fact, I fell off the stage into the lap of a middle aged woman in the front row. I remember she had enormous breasts which, fortunately, I refrained from groping.

I investigated artistically oriented schools and came up with a California college called the California Institute of Arts and Crafts, or Cal Arts, for short. It was less about the school than the idea of not freezing my balls off in another East Coast winter.

I auditioned for Cal Arts as an actor in their NY office and was somehow accepted in the acting program. My dad agreed to send me and so off I went to sunny California to continue what was rapidly becoming a non-career.

California was better than I thought it would be. The college was located in Valencia, about thirty miles north of Los Angeles, on a pristine campus. Everything was better about California. There were fruit trees outside my dorm. Real oranges, lemons, and grapefruits!

This was amazing to me. I knew fruits grew somewhere but to see them actually growing was awesome.

Except now, in California, I was around more accomplished actors, people who were serious about acting careers. California is where all actors migrate, like birds, as if they by some instinct.

Many of these aspiring actors were nuts. They made the actors in Boston seem normal by comparison. Every other day ambulances were pulling up to campus and taking these freaks away due to mental breakdowns or drug overdoses.

I decided to switch to the directing program. The second that I did I felt a huge weight lift. I knew I had made the right choice. These days every other student at Cal Arts wants to be a director, but in those days it was a singular choice.

One night I had a dream that I would fall in love with a beautiful blond, haired, blue-eyed girl. She would be like the girl on the Swiss Maid cocoa wrapper. The next day I was in the cafeteria when the girl of my dreams walked by the table. I introduced myself and told her about my dream. I expected her to throw herself into my arms. She looked at me like I was crazy and sped away.

I was persistent. Her name was Sheila and before long we were dating. It wasn't like Boston, where a date consisted of two Quaaludes, a session in bed, and a roast beef sandwich at Arby's. We went to theater, on walks, and fine dinners. Sheila was a dancer and had studied to be a dancer her entire life. She was the most beautiful woman I had ever met, inside and out. I was living the dream, a dream that had become my reality.

Even though I felt lucky, based on my past experiences I was waiting for some calamity, some disaster, to wreck my newfound happiness.

CHAPTER 13: CAL ARTS

For a while things went well. Sheila was the woman of my dreams. She was my muse, too. I decided to make directing my mission. Except there was no directing department at Cal Arts. I sort of established my own identity. Several of the professors liked my imagination and nurtured my choice.

I read a Terrence McNally play that I liked. I cast and directed it. I thought about adding a scene that featured Sheila dancing, but when I mentioned it to the panel of professors, they looked at me like I was crazy, so I dropped the idea.

I loved the thrill of putting ideas into action, which is what directing is to me. The show went over well and I was on my way. Christmas break we went up to Canada to visit Sheila's parents. We shared a train car with an older couple. At a rest stop the old guy clutched his chest, keeled over and died. Sheila was freaked. I thought, well, this is how it goes in my life.

Sheila came from a big family. Her parents were great, everybody was so nice and... normal. I could barely recognize normal, not with my upbringing.

We spent the summer together. I proposed to Sheila. Things were looking rosy. I entered my third year of college filled with the desire to direct something special.

I directed a play here and there but then, read a piece called "The Murder" by William Inge. Yes, I thought, this spooky play is about the dark demons that seemed to be following me. Perhaps my execution of this nugget would expunge those evil spirits.

I poured my soul into the project. Day after day, I directed the actors with every nuance of Inge's words echoing in my soul. It was mounted as the featured piece during in the Cal Arts Festival. Audiences were enthralled and I was lauded.

Because of such directorial work, my degree was accelerated and I graduated a year early. I felt like a big shot, I who had directed a total of maybe ten plays in college.

Shortly after graduation, Sheila and I started to grow apart. Maybe we didn't have the safe shelter of college to protect our love. In any event, we finally ended it. I guess I found her too normal. I needed more craziness, more insanity in my life. I was certainly soon to find it.

CHAPTER 14: NEW BEGINNINGS

After graduating from Cal Arts with a Bachelor of Fine Arts in theater, I waited to become the next hot film director in Hollywood. I expected producers to beat thier feet to my door. Boy, was I delusional. The truth was I knew nothing about film. So I did the next logical thing and got hired as a runner/production assistant for various movie and television production companies. At the same time, I started hanging out in the editing bay and learned the art of film editing. I soon worked my way up from an assistant editor to a full editor. Although my skill was marginal, I heard about a small family production house looking for an editor. Thanks to a friend, I got the job.

It was here that I wrote my first documentary called CREATURES OF THE AMAZON, a two hour syndicated documentary profiling the natives and the animals that populate our planet. Since I had never been to the Amazon, editors cutting this special would send me finished segments without sound. I would study the footage, go to the library and hunt for facts and tales about the Amazon, and apply them. I soon had wall to wall narration.

During the recording session, the boss started screaming that the movie was over-written. I had one chance: to take my pen and make cuts, or face being fired. I re-edited my narration while everyone was out to lunch. When my boss started the afternoon recording session, he was pleased. The gods were with me as the newly edited version worked well.

The truth was that I had no idea what I was doing but I pulled it off while getting a crash course in narrative film writing. I learned that when you put words to a picture, the words had to add color. I learned not to write what I was seeing, but find scenic bridges between the words and images.

I was in my early twenties feeling immortal, insane, and ready to die for my craft. Sometimes, you have to be careful what you wish for.

Over the next couple of years the owner's son and I became friends and collaborators on several projects. One day, several Japanese executives came to us and asked if we could make a documentary about death. They wanted us to capture the horror of death and the more macabre the better.

It was the moment I had been waiting for. This was the calling that had begun in a coffin and extended into my young adulthood. I felt I had cultivated insights few mortals might have. This death movie was my destiny.

After the meeting, the owner's son came up with the title and I came up with the concept: the story of a pathologist who over time has compiled a library of death. The movie would simply chronicle his experiences.

I was inspired by THE HELLSTROM CHRONICLES, a movie about an etymologist who believes that insects will destroy mankind and take over the earth. The film was shot as a documentary and was so believable that I was convinced it was true. As the end credits rolled, I discovered the documentary was fabrication and had twisted the truth by combining fact with fiction. I had the insight that this is what I wanted to do with our movie.

The first thing we had to do was to write up a treatment. We mixed real ideas with stories fueled by our own imagination. We had no idea how we would produce our segments, but we agreed that the more shocking and bloody, the better.

CHAPTER 15: CASTING DR. GROSS
AND THE RECURRING DREAM

We had to find someone who could play our pathologist. We met with many actors, but none had the unique quality we were seeking. What that quality was, we weren't sure of, but we'd "know it when we see it."

One day I spotted that quality and it was the face of death itself.

I remember walking down the hallway when I observed a tall, skinny guy dressed in black, smoking a slim cigarette, and slouching toward me. He was in his early forties. Behind his glasses there was doom in his eyes. I immediately knew he was our pathologist, whom I decided to name Dr Gross. I went to my partner and told him I had found our on-camera host. My partner took one look at the guy, shuddered, and agreed

A day later we met with the fellow whose name was Michael Carr. He was not overly interested in participating. I handed Mike some copy and asked him to read it. Carr asked us to leave the room so he could study the copy. About ten minutes later, he opened the door and asked, "Who wrote this shit?" I raised my hand and Carr laughed.

Carr read us the copy. His reading glasses were cockeyed. He would grunt and groan in a deathly monotone as he said the words. It was like watching a hangman prepare the noose or the

Angel of Death sharpen his scythe. I intuitively knew this was a role of a lifetime for Mike and on some perverse level he knew it, too.

Over the next few days, I wrote up a back story for Mike's character. We created a whole bio about this crazy pathologist. What I needed was the reason he was so fascinated with death. What would compel a pathologist to maintain his own library of death? The answer was not easy until I came up with the idea that our doctor had recurring nightmares about death complete with perpetual funerals.

To create the dream sequence, we filmed a bunch of us dressed in suits carrying an open coffin. The girl in the coffin, an office secretary, was dressed in white. She looked angelic and scary at the same time.When we filmed the closing of the coffin, we kept her inside too long. When we lifted her out she was unconscious. It was touch and go, but we revived her. She was almost our first face of death. Maybe we should have heeded the warning.

We debated if maybe the project was too risky. We decided to go forth. It was now time to film the segments I had concocted as part of Dr. Gross's library of death

CHAPTER 16: THE SLAUGHTERHOUSES

One area of death we had to explore was life in the slaughterhouse. We first filmed at a slaughterhouse in Vernon, California... the place was a massive killing machine. Thousands of cattle were killed every day. There is a certain smell of death in such a place that permeates your clothes and body. Weeks after filming in this place some of my clothes still smelled like death.

The killing process is swift. A stun gun is placed in the back of the steer's head. This swift blow knocks the cattle out, and it slides down to the butchers waiting to cut it up

In the kosher slaughtering process, a Rabbi says a prayer as he slits the cow's throat and watches the animal bleed to death. The workers are always sharpening their knives. I asked many of them what it was like to do this day after day. One said, "Someone's got to do it so it might as well be me." As the dead animal moves down the conveyor belt, every part of its body is butchered.

Another place we filmed was a lamb slaughterhouse in a town in Northern California called Petaluma. There was one experience that I'll never forget. One of the guys came up to me and said. "Put me in your movie."

"Why should I?" I replied. Without saying a word, he bit the ear off a living lamb and spit it out. The lamb's screams reverberate in my head to this day. I never did put him in the film.

The way they slaughter a lamb is to stick it in the back of the head with a stun pole and apply an electric charge that paralyzes the animal. The lamb is then connected to a conveyor belt and butchered within minutes. One of the guys led me to a pen filled with about 20 lambs. He handed me the stun pole and said, "Come on, Gringo, they're all yours." In the next moment, I went into a frenzy and stunned the lambs. As they were placed on the line, my hands were shaking. At that moment I swore I would never eat meat again.

Three hours later we went to lunch and had lamb kabobs. How quickly we forget. I think none of us wanted to appear fearful. How stupid was that?

We also shot in a chicken slaughterhouse. This place was also a massive killing machine. The chickens are placed on a conveyor belt upside down to disorient them. Their throats are then slit by workers on the line. The next stop is the de-feathering process where feathers are plucked in seconds. Then the birds are cut up and stored in a giant freezer. Walking through the freezer filled with thousands of freshly killed chickens had its own smell of death. I wonder if Colonel Sanders ever saw the inside of one of them.

One intimate slaughter took place at a crew member's aunt's house. She was slaughtering a rooster for dinner and let us film her home grown process. She sharpened her axe then placed the rooster on a butcher block. Several seconds later she chopped off the bird's head. The rooster danced around the barnyard for what seemed like minutes When the bird was finally dead, the woman drained the blood and asked if we would like to stay for dinner. We took a rain check.

When filming in slaughterhouses one could sense the fear of the animals. Perhaps animals too had the fear of the unknown. I will never forget seeing what it takes to feed the hungry masses and how we hide the horror and the process behind our food.

CHAPTER 17: THE MONKEY BRAINS

It was now time to try to mix the real with the imagined and make it appear seamless. This was the true challenge of the film's concept and the segment that followed the harsh reality of animal slaughter was among our most daring. In fact, the segment is perhaps the most controversial in the original FACES OF DEATH.

I had come up with the idea of a restaurant somewhere in the Middle East where diners kill a monkey at their table and eat its brains. I had read it was supposed to be a religious experience. After doing a bit more research, I found that people do eat monkey brains but the monkeys are never brought live to the table.

Our fictional restaurant did all that and more. We hired a monkey trainer with his most tractable monkey. Our makeup team sculpted a duplicate head that the waiter would open. We built a special table with a round opening so the animal's head could be secured as the table's centerpiece. We also constructed foam mallets that looked real.

We found a Moroccan restaurant in Long Beach with a belly dancer.

The owner of the restaurant and his wife sat at the table with two older crew members. The four looked like tourists out for a special meal in a foreign country.

The table was set and we were ready to go. We had to film

in one take due to the insistence of the animal trainer. We began with the belly dancer gyrating her hips. The tourists tipped her and one the men slapped her ass. Typical ugly Americans. Next up was the monkey and his trainer, both dressed in Middle East garb.

When the trainer placed the monkey's head into the table opening the animal freaked. The trainer tried to calm the monkey down with little success. The diners were told to hit the monkey on the head as if to kill it. Although the foam mallets were harmless the monkey cried out as if he was being slaughtered. He was a damn good actor. We shot with three cameras and once we got the footage and reaction shots we replaced the monkey with a perfectly sculpted double.

One of our makeup guys cracked open the phony skull and it looked like real brains. Our diners showed a range of emotions as they dipped spoons inside the head and nibbled on the "brains," which were red-dyed cauliflower. If you looked closely you could see a nail holding down the bloody cauliflower. Fortunately, most people weren't that observant.

We had sound problems, so we looped the scene and four of the crew supplied the voices. When we reviewed the footage we knew we were onto something. The monkey scene seemed as genuine as the Vernon slaughter house. To this day, this is the one segment that people swear is real.

CHAPTER 18: ANIMAL FIGHTS

As long as we were descending into the profane, I had the idea to do a segment about dog fighting. We put out the word and after several negotiations and thousands in cash, we went to Compton to film a fight. We went to a rundown neighborhood where roof top lookouts with binoculars kept their eyes open for cops.

Two pit bulls were brought out and they lunged at one another. The hatred was real. We told our contact that we didn't need a dog to die. Our plan was to squirt mock blood on the dogs to make things look much worse than they were. The dogs were placed in the ring and they went at it. I thought for sure one of them would be killed. The trainers were tough guys and these dogs were even tougher. We kept squirting phony blood over the dogs. One dog collapsed from exhaustion, but staggered to his feet seconds later. We stopped the fight before he died. We had plenty of fight footage and it was a perfect place for us to stop filming. We could freeze-frame the dog that collapsed and give the illusion that the dog had died. Besides, some of the locals were getting too close to our equipment truck and it was time to get out of Compton.

We also traveled to Leon, Mexico to film cock fights. Unfortunately, I came down with "tourista" in the middle of filming. While the other guys filmed, I wandered around the parking lot shitting and puking. I thought I would die and wondered if my passing would make an interesting segment. I had been feeling funky the whole day and I knew something was up. The night before we played poker and drank too many shots of tequila and ate pork burritos. I had ignored the rule that while in Mexico be careful what you eat and drink.

I paid no attention and now I was paying for it big time. Later that evening our guide gave me some pills and I was back in 24 hours ready to eat and drink everything… well, almost everything.

CHAPTER 19: THE PSYCHIC MARIA MORENO

A friend told me about this amazing psychic in East Los Angeles. I thought we could do a story about life after death. When I met her, she went into a trance and screamed that I was a murderer. She had tuned into the slaughter houses and the blood and death I had experienced. Once she believed I was not a killer, she calmed down and went into a deeper trance, where she proceeded to tell me intimate facts about my family, friends, and my career.

The only thing that troubled me was that as I was leaving her office, she warned me that when one draws closer to death, there is often no escape.

"This film you are doing," she whispered, "Be careful!"

I sent my parents to Maria. She tuned into my Dad's best friend who died on the battlefield of Normandy. I invited her to be in our movie, but she declined, telling me that her powers were given to her not to make her famous or rich but to help people in need. She did tell us that our film would be groundbreaking. Once again, how right she was!

CHAPTER 20: THE JUMPER

When we started to produce FACES OF DEATH, we knew that film libraries and news outfits and stringers (freelance camera men) could provide us with provocative stories that were turned down because of their graphic content. Of course that was exactly what we were looking for.

One of my favorite places to go was UPI, a world wide news producer. Vince O'Reilly ran the library and the two guys who pulled footage were crazy Jamaicans. Whenever they saw me they said, "Yo, mon, the Doctor Of Death be in the house."

The footage they found was incredible. From car crashes to natural disasters, they had it all. I would get weekly updates if bizarre footage came through the door. A great find was a story we called "The Jumper."

This was real footage of a middle aged woman standing on the ledge of a twenty story building. The cameraman got there just as she was about to jump. Three minutes later the woman jumped to her death.

After studying this footage, we saw an opportunity to increase the suspense by inter-cutting cops and fireman running up the stairs trying to save her.

We intercut this race against time until she jumped. After her body smashed to the pavement, the real cameraman stopped shooting. We added inserts of our own photographer crossing the street to discover the lifeless woman, her brains seeping out of her head. Everything matched perfectly and people couldn't tell the difference between the actual footage and our recreated shots. It was eerie to watch because it seemed so real. This distraught woman had nowhere to turn and her demons were out in full force. I wonder what her last thoughts were right before she jumped. One thing is for sure, she was unhappy about something and she ran out of answers. I could never jump to my death. I'm too terrified of heights… although I've heard it said that it is the fear of jumping, not the height, that terrifies people.

We had a mad German composing our music and just as the woman was about to jump, you heard a voice say "One, two, a one, two, three, four." And then, right on cue, the woman jumped. This became my favorite music cue since it added a new level of horror to The Jumper.

CHAPTER 21: ALLIGATORS

I never liked the original gator footage we planned for FACES OF DEATH. I thought the whole incident looked stiff.

We hired park rangers to handle the gators and work as stunt men. What we wanted was for one of the rangers to get pulled into the water by a gator and wrestle with the creature until his partner yanks him back into the boat in the nick of time.

The gator was thrashing about and our ranger looked like he was in trouble. The problem was, the gator's mouth was tied shut and although it was moving it never looked like the ranger would be bitten. Although the tail of a gator can kill, and an alligator will destroy a human without hesitation, something in the scene was missing.

I remember asking one of the rangers why he chose to work with these vicious reptiles. "I love the action," he said. Both men had fingers and toes missing. This is one club I'd never want to join.

One day I was over at UPI in New York. After the rather prosaic gator scene, I felt I was losing my way. I was looking through the library for something deadly when one of the Jamaicans showed me footage of a skydiver whose parachute never opened. But as he dive bombed to earth, the skydiver fell out of frame and you never saw him meet his maker.

When I screened this in Los Angeles I had an inspiration:

what if I had the unlucky skydiver land in the alligator pond? I knew I had hit on a great idea for a segment.

We found the perfect alligator park in rural Florida. The owner agreed not to feed the gators so they would be extra aggressive. We matched the skydiver caught on film with a dummy stuffed with a fresh killed pig

Three of us were positioned on a dock which extended into pond. I was holding the battery belts while our other guys were shooting. Several workers from the gator farm were ready to throw the dummy into the pond from a winch 25 feet above the water to make it seem as he was falling from the sky. Once the dummy was in the water, they gave us guide ropes tied to the dummy so we wanted to move it. We poured pig blood into the water to get the gators primed for flesh.

The handlers warned us to let go of the rope if we felt severe tugging. I was scared shitless. I knew if one of the gators yanked the dummy the wrong way, I could be pulled into the water.

The dummy was dropped, hit the water, and the gators attacked. The guide ropes tied to the dummy nearly dragged us into the pond. Watching these creatures consume their meal was frightening. One alligator that kept staring at me and it wasn't the look of love.

In the end, we pulled it off. We matched the falling skydiver and the alligator bloodlust perfectly. I was proud of my work. Over the years this segment has had many loyal fans.

An alligator will attack when the time is right. Humans stand little chance. The alligator attack images sent tingles down my spine.

CHAPTER 22: FLESH EATING CULT

I always thought a flesh eating cult would be a good idea. I thought of the segment after watching footage of a Tennessee Cult praying to Jesus while holding rattlesnakes all over their bodies. The ceremony ended with several members being bitten and going into shock. The other members continued to pray harder and louder.

The idea behind the FLESH EATING CULT was that our crew would be allowed to film a secret ceremony where our make-believe cult would consume a human. Our cult would believe human flesh gives them immortality, with every organ having a different power. As a boner, I mean bonus, the sexual energy from eating the dead would be tremendous and the ceremony end in an orgy.

I cast myself as the leader of the cult and several of the male cult members were friends from Cal Arts. Our casting call went out and we saw thirty women who stripped for us. There are great truths to be told about the casting couch. I almost forgot about the film. I started believing the women liked me because I was the head of a cult and not a film-maker!

Indeed, for those moments when the cameras rolled we were transformed into our own demented cult. When it came time to slit open the body of a thoroughly frightened crew member, I was given a very sharp knife. One of the makeup guys showed me where to press. When I started he screamed and twitched. I put less pressure on the knife and the rest went perfectly. We substituted a fake body. Our cult moved in and gnawed on the bloody flesh, which was flank steak and theater blood. As the group became more primal, we started kissing and licking each other and one girl shook with a real orgasm. No one heard the word cut because we were so having so much fun.

CHAPTER 23: THE ELECTROCUTION

While I was recovering from almost dying from excessive copulation as head of the cult, I was going through some papers when a copy of HUSTLER magazine appeared in my inbox. On the cover page was an article called "The Real Truth Behind Electrocutions." This was an amazing article that took you step by step through an electrocution. I was blown away by this information. I knew we could recreate this and people would buy it. The article became my outline.

Several pieces would have to be put together to make this and we weren't going to take no for an answer. While our team was building an electric chair, we got permission to shoot background at a prison in Chino. We hired a talented production designer to recreate a cell to hold the electric chair. This was constructed at a warehouse in East Los Angeles

Casting our actor was easy because my neighbor was a tortured soul who looked like he was on Death Row. From the moment I cast him, he was always improving his character by getting more and more depressed contemplating his imminent execution.

A few weeks later, we were ready to go. Our background in Chino was completed. We moved to our set in the warehouse. Our makeup team ran tubes from corners of my neighbor's eyes and mouth.

Now came the big moment, once everyone exited the cell.

You could see the frightened face of the prisoner. When I called action, our prisoner lurched forward and his whole body jerked and shook until foam, which was Crest toothpaste, poured out of his mouth and nose, and fake blood dripped down his cheeks. He convulsed for several minutes and we shot it again for insurance.

To this day people think this segment is real. We were proud of this sequence. Everyone stepped up and worked as a team. When everyone shares the same vision they add their own creative touch to a film.

Now that we had completed the electric chair, we were eager to film another kind of mock execution. The gas chamber was a logical choice. After much research, we located one at Arizona State Prison.

We managed to talk our way into the prison and the guards, who had all worked on death row, couldn't have been more helpful. Our "actor" was a real inmate. The guards showed us how the gas chamber works, from the moment the prisoner is strapped into his chair, to the deadly gas pellets which are dropped into an acid solution that releases the gas.

We asked a guard why he volunteered to work this section of the prison. The guard collected his thoughts and said "The guys on death row committed horrendous crimes. Our job is to keep the peace. When a prisoner learns the day and time of his execution we help him find forgiveness within himself and the people he has hurt. A guard can never get too close to a condemned man because a man on death row has nothing to lose."

Later that day we shot the gas chamber and it went perfectly. Not as good as the electrocution, but it was still quite compelling. I thought about filming a hanging, but decided I had seen enough of men killing their fellow humans.

Prison is one of those places that you don't want to spend more time in than necessary. It's a place of harsh realities where time more often than not stands still.

CHAPTER 24: THE SHOOTOUT

I figured we needed a good police shootout. I wanted the death scene to be reminiscent of Warren Beatty's death in Bonnie and Clyde. Anybody who has ever seen that will never forget it. We found a cul-de-sac in on a small street in Hollywood. We got a permit from the film commission and were off to the races.

I had envisioned the scene as a hostage standoff. We shot with six cameras, mostly handheld. I decided to shoot in real time to capture the immediacy of a hostage crisis.

What with the cops, criminal, hostages and so forth, there were lots of moving parts. I had never directed so many people, but I storyboarded what I needed and the rest I just did by the seat of my pants.

The day of the shoot I rehearsed the segment with the cops and the crazed killer who had taken a family hostage. I just hoped my direction would work. We had one more rehearsal and then it was time to go.

Everybody took their places. When I yelled action, cop cars zoomed into position and I filmed the killer in the house screaming from a window and shooting wildly. A SWAT team showed up and they took up places around the perimeter. They blasted gas canisters into the house and the killer came charging out. He jittered like a puppet on strings until, after being peppered with at least twenty rounds, he collapsed. I swear, it fulfilled my vision of Clyde Barrow's death in the movie.

The cops raced into the house where they discovered the entire family shot to death. The cops put their hands over the camera lens and we faded to black.

Later that night, we all went out for a drink. We had done it again. Everyone had been ready to take that extra step. We had formed an incredible team. We even got shots of helicopters flying over the house.

There are times in your life where you feel like you've accomplished something. In life you must seize the moment. On the day of the shoot we did exactly that. It seemed as if an angel was watching over us. I was to discover it was the Angel of Death.

CHAPTER 25: THE MORGUE.

We managed to get permission to shoot in the LA COUNTY MORGUE for several days. This was truly one of the most bizarre places I have ever seen and that still is true 30 years later.

Anyone who dies an unnatural death is sent to the morgue. I remember the first tour. As we walked down the hallway there was one guy with a rope still around his neck and a 25 year old male whose body was twisted like a pretzel. We found out he had been in a head-on collision while riding his motorcycle and wasn't wearing a helmet.

We walked down the long hallway until we reached the automatic doors to discover seven autopsies going on simultaneously. From babies to the elderly and those in between, we saw a row of bodies lying on cold, hard metal tables.

The place smelled like a rotten deli. The workers told us that for their very sanity they had to find some levity in this dark place. One guy confided that he put on disco music and danced with female corpses after dark.

We went to the break room which was right around the corner from the dead bodies. I tried to eat my lunch, but the stench of death overwhelmed me. I pushed my bologna sandwich into the trash. One of the workers told me I'd be fine in a few weeks.

Some of the highlights of the tour included a visit to the

embalming room and a trip to a massive walk-in refrigerator that held 100 dead bodies waiting for their final resting place.

We shot for several days inside the morgue and even interviewed Thomas Noguchi. He was the coroner for Los Angeles county and performed autopsies on Robert Kennedy and Marilyn Monroe. He lent great credibility to our film. I wonder what he thought when and if he saw that his interview came after the segment in which I was the leader of a flesh eating cult.

As I looked at the morgue footage, I wrote a poem about death that Dr. Gross read over images of the dead bodies, each with a unique look on his face. What amazed me the most about this experience is that death takes the spirit out of us and we are just shells.

One day that I walked into the empty autopsy room and thought: is this what death is about? Where do we go after that final moment?

One thing is for sure, no one gets out alive. If that's true maybe the old adage applies that says "the second time is the charm."

Now, years later, I wonder if there is a second time. I've spent a great part of my life studying death and I have yet to understand the final curtain. I simply hope my death is quick and painless.

CHAPTER 26: THE MIDDLE EASTERN BEHEADING

I got a depressing phone call about two weeks after the Noguchi interview. One of my prep school classmates had been brutally beaten and beheaded by his gay lover in a West Hollywood apartment. It was a big story for a day or two. Although I thought I was finished with executions, in my classmate's honor I decided to do a beheading segment.

In real life, though, who would film a beheading? This was long before radical Islamists aired filmed beheadings as a terrorist ploy.

I came up with the idea that a freelance cameraman working in the Middle East would covertly shoot an execution, nearly paying for it with his life.

The first thing we had to do was find a location that resembled The Sahara. After some location scouting, we found a patch of desert that had been used by Hollywood for over thirty years, in Yuma.

We set up a Bedouin camp with primitive tents. We found a tree trunk where the beheading was to take place. After cutting a deal with the Yuma Arizona Chamber of Commerce, we cast several Indians from a local tribe and dressed them in robes and Bedouin headwear.

We selected one of our crew members to be "beheaded." Our

make-up guys quickly produced a superb model of his head. They did a great job with the monkey head and they came through again. The model head was connected to a torso secured by a harness. When the sword went through the head's neck, the head would hopefully topple into a basket.

Our "victim" was lead over to the tree trunk. A member of our effects gang, the "executioner", was prepared to bring a scimitar down to within less than an inch of our actor's neck. This was a one take deal which we shot with three cameras.

It was hot. Everybody was sweating. By noon the desert was a blazing 114 degrees. We told the cameramen not to shoot too close so nobody would notice flaws in our dummy.

We shot several angles of our Bedouin Camp and then set up the beheading.

Our "executioner" was very nervous. He was covered with sweat. He was afraid his hands were so slippery that he might cut our actor's head off. For a second I thought about stopping the shoot. For some reason I decided to continue.

We called action and our "victim" was led to the chopping block and forced to kneel. There was no room for error. One of the guys blindfolded him. The executioner raised his razor sharp sword. Held it in the air. Brought it down. I held my breath. It stopped a millimeter before the man's neck.

We intercut it with the dummy footage. The executioner's sword sliced through the dummy's neck like butter. The head rolled right into the basket.

After we finished packing up, I climbed up a sand dune and checked out the beauty of this stark, unique place. I was hoping to see Peter O'Toole riding his stallion across the desert. Although that never happened, the Yuma desert was a great place to find serenity, despite the brutal heat, and a scorpion bite that crippled me for three days.

CHAPTER 27: THE BEAR

In many horrible accidents, the most grisly and painful deaths occur unexpectedly, and often when people are having the time of their lives.

I thought of circumstances in which people would be having a good time. There is nothing better than a pleasant vacation. How could I introduce horror and death into a vacation?

I thought about a husband and wife innocently filming from their car in a woodsy place like Yosemite. A bear would wander into the frame. The wife would be enamored of the bear's "cuteness." It looks "like a teddy bear," she would tell her husband. She convinces him that the bear is harmless. Against his better judgment, the man gets out of the car. Of course, the bear attacks the husband even as he continues filming.

To put an exclamation point on the scene, I thought it would be really frightening if during the attack, the bear bites the man's arm off and scampers away with the appendage in its jaws.

I found a bear trainer and pitched him our idea and wondered whether this was possible and could be done safely. The trainer said Jake, his huge black bear, was usually okay, but warned us when you're working with bears there are no guarantees.

Several weeks later, we were in Squim, Washington shooting the sequence. The couple we cast was our production secretary and her husband. They looked like perfect all American tourists. We shot all the background we needed except for the bear attack.

My partner pre-rehearsed the couple. They went over and met Jake, the bear, and the trainer. The husband was very apprehensive. I told him there was nothing to worry about, that the bear was a pro and did everything the trainer asked him to do. I didn't tell him about the trainer's "no guarantees" warning.

When we started filming, everything went on cue. As the husband approached the bear with his camera, the trainer got Jake to stand on its back legs and roar. After another cue, Jake pulled the man to the ground. The wife started screaming. The bear stood over the husband and roared again. Then the bear lunged, rose up, and in its jaws was the man's "arm," which was actually a prosthetic filled with sugary treats and sausages.

When the woman saw the bear tear her husband's arm, she screamed uncontrollably. She really freaked. I realized I had forgotten to tell her about the fake arm.

Unconcerned about her screams, the bear munched happily on the sausage arm and cantered off with the thing in its mouth. I tell you, it happened EXACTLY as I dreamed it up.

The wife's near breakdown was something we did not expect. Our production secretary was brilliant and her performance made the story convincing.

Not that it wasn't convincing enough. When we came over to congratulate the husband, we found him unconscious and bleeding from a huge gash in his shoulder. The bear had actually attacked him. Twenty pints of blood and two weeks in a hospital later, he managed to recover.

Fear can sometimes drive one to death. We have so many ways to die and yet we have no idea what happens when we face the final curtain. After hearing the secretary's blood curdling screams in the edit bay weeks later, I really think she was one step away from being scared to death.

CHAPTER 28: THE MUMMIES

When it came to horror movies, as a kid mummies had always frightened me. There was something about an entity returning from the dead to exact revenge that was beyond horrifying. So I decided to do a segment about mummies.

We went back to Mexico. This time I brought my own food and water. I was going to film the mummies of Guanajuato. In this beautiful city in Central Mexico, we were to discover an entire museum filled with mummies that were hundreds of years old. It is believed that the rich soil contained minerals that mummified the bodies.

We first filmed in the cemetery. It was filled with headstones hundreds of years old. In another part of the cemetery, the graves were dug up so that archeologists could unearth perfectly preserved mummies.

Then we filmed inside the museum. There were dozens of mummies: men, women, and children preserved for centuries in the earth. Some faces wore grins while others were frozen in fear and or pain. It felt like each mummy had its own moment with death. We turned on our lights and took close shots of the mummies' faces. We got so close we could smell the scent of death. It was a musky smell and some mummies smelled more than others. This is one place where ghosts and mummies are best friends. I wondered if they came to life in the middle of the night. There were rumors that several people who work with the mummies suffered untimely deaths.

By the end of the day, we put away our cameras and went out for drinks. After several shots of tequila, we asked our guide about the mummies and the supernatural. Our guide paused for a moment and told us the mummies came back to life in his dreams. They would chase him and he would manage to out run them. I asked him what would happen if the mummies caught him. Our guide got very quiet. He looked to the heavens, made a sign of the cross, and brought the full bottle of tequila to his lips. I never brought up my question again.

That night, I dreamed that I was being chased by mummies. Only this time they caught me and were about to eat me. I woke up in a cold sweat and finally fell back asleep. I never dreamed about the mummies again and prayed they weren't dreaming about me.

CHAPTER 29: SELF-IMMOLATION

One image that always stuck in my mind was when monks set themselves on fire to protest the Vietnamese war. What made the images so horrific was how stoic the monks were as their bodies crackled and burned. There was never a scream, just the sound of flesh melting. When the fire was extinguished, the burnt monks were long dead but with an enigmatic smile on their faces.

We all agreed that this type of death had to be in our movie. I came up with the idea of a bunch of protesters marching in front of a nuclear reactor. They wanted the facility to shut down, but their cries were ignored. In my conception, one of the protesters would kneel before the plant, squirt lighter fluid on his clothes, and set himself on fire. The other protesters would try to save him but fail to do so. I wanted our human fireball to die as peacefully as the monks.

The key, as I had learned from the wife screaming in the bear scene, was NOT to tell the other protesters that one of the marchers was going to immolate himself. That way, when it happened, their horror would be real and lend credibility to the segment.

We hired a stuntman known for lighting himself on fire. He had done it hundreds of times. I wondered if his insurance agent knew his true occupation. We went over the details. He prepared a special fireproof suit and various emollients that would withstand the inferno. We dressed one of our crew members in a security outfit who would try to save the protester with a fire extinguisher.

It was time for the big moment. The protesters were marching peacefully. Suddenly our stuntman burst from the line of marchers. He kneeled before the power plant and squirted the lighter fluid on himself. He put a match to his arm. He was soon consumed in flames as his fellow protesters looked on in horror.

This was great! Just like I imagined it! The stuntman was screaming. I thought he was doing a great acting job. Almost as good as the wife in the bear scene. Then I heard the words "PUT ME OUT, PUT ME OUT!"

The stuntman was clearly in big trouble. Our security guard raced in and doused the fire. We were to discover that the stuntman's arm was truly on fire as there was a small tear on his special fireproof suit. It was the first time it had ever happened it him.

In spite of that, we got the footage we needed. What started as a simple protest ended in immolation. None of our protestors had any idea that one of their fellow dissenters was going to light himself up. When it happened those were real screams of terror.

I admire conviction and fearlessness. During our lives, there is that point where you have to put it all on the line even it means your death in the process. That's why I always say live with courage…die with honor.

Nevertheless, it was not lost on me that this was the fourth person who had almost died during the filming of our movie about death. I wondered if and when death would catch up with us.

CHAPTER 30: STOCK FOOTAGE
FROM AROUND THE WORLD

When we began pre-production we knew that stock footage would bring us great images. What we found far exceeded my expectations. From auto accidents to concentration camp footage from WWII to the airline crash of a PSA commuter jet… It was all out there and after doing a lot of research, we were able to stay within our budget.

If we weren't dealing with the big film libraries, we were running ads in alternative magazines and in newspapers across the country. I remember flying to Minnesota to meet with a stringer who had dozens of reels of gruesome accident footage. The guy was proud of the footage. He described the stories behind the images, telling me that the closer he got to accident victims, dead or alive, the more his heart pumped with adrenalin. He said it was better than sex. As I listened to this guy babble, I had the feeling that if he wasn't shooting accident footage he would have made a fine serial killer.

An example of gruesome images was a PSA jet which crashed into a residential neighborhood. A stringer witnessed the crash from just blocks away. He ran into his house, grabbed his camera, and started filming.

When he arrived on the scene, parts of the jet were still burning. The ground was strewn with severed arms, legs, and smoking mounds of flesh. A middle class neighborhood had been transformed into a giant morgue. The stringer said that the stench of death filled the air and he was still tormented by the horror. When I first saw the footage, it moved me in a very deep way. Men, women, and children, all innocent, and yet judged guilty by an unseen hand. I wondered what thoughts they had as the out-of-control jet plummeted to earth. I'm certain every human emotion was played out.

The stringer told us that after several explosions, there was an eerie silence and he swore that he could feel electricity surrounding him. I said maybe it was the innocent souls moving on. The stringer looked at me and slowly nodded. You could see the anguish in his eyes.

I am sure the stringer would have many sleepless nights as he stood in death's doorway.

CHAPTER 31: THE DEAD BODY

The ending of our movie was a woman giving birth. We cast another neighbor. She had milky, white skin and her face was wholesome. She had a farm girl look. We shot the birth and spread a little theater blood on the baby. It was another great shoot. My neighbor looked radiant and the baby even cried on cue.

The next shot was of mother and child in a hot tub. This was corny but after the brutal ride we had given our audience, I was certain the juxtaposition would be startling. People often laugh at the ending, probably out of relief that something horrible isn't happening to the woman and her child.

Our final shot was of mother holding the baby and walking along the shore. The light was golden and the waves perfect. Mother and child were peaceful. This was an ideal shoot until we heard screaming. We rushed about 50 yards down the beach to find a young male surfer whose limp body floated back and forth. The guy had one shoe on. We figured he overdosed and drowned.

Moments later the life guard arrived and covered the body. We hung out and helped the coroners place the body into their van.

We felt strange at dinner that night. Even when we were celebrating life we were stalked by death. Was the dead surfer another sign that we had overstepped the boundary between life and death?

We got drunk. As the booze loosened us up, we laughed about the incident. That was our way of dealing with the disturbing reality of another lifeless body crossing the line. He was such a young guy, too, reminding me that death has no favorites.

CHAPTER 32: MY FACES OF DEATH ROLES

Since I had started off as an actor, and had experience, I knew this movie would be the perfect place for me to create a variety of characters. The day we filmed the FLESH EATING CULT we rehearsed the action several times. We shot with three cameras and would have only one shot of the body being cut open.

As I already revealed, the guy I portrayed was a Charlie Manson type who manipulated the members of his cult by keeping them high on LSD. Once I performed that role, my appetite was whetted. I wanted to appear in more segments.

We debated the sense in this. Would people recognize me from one segment to the next? Obviously, we were in the business of creating a believable alternate reality. If I was spotted in several scenes, the film's credibility would go out the window.

We decided to risk it. Maybe after playing the cult leader I thought I was God and could do anything.

It was actually me playing the the speed freak in the Bonnie and Clyde hostage-shooting scene! I was wired to about 20 squibs which are small explosive charges made to simulate bullets entering the flesh. I was fearful when I was wired up. But I went for it, as I did with all the segments of FACES OF DEATH.

I exited the store with my two hostages. I used them as a shield but the marksman had an open shot and hit me in the shoulder.

The pain from the exploding squib made me release the hostages. The cops had an open shot. As the exploding squibs blasted me, I twisted and turned with real pain until I fell to the ground, grateful to pretend to be dead. That night, I put ice on my black and blue chest. One thing was for sure, if I ever had to wear another squib it wouldn't be in this lifetime.

In my final role I played a rapist. To play this character I slicked back my hair and wore a mustache. A tape of me raping and killing a girl was shown on tape in the court room. When the judge refused bail, I smirked and gave him the finger. The judge had some sheriffs remove me from the courtroom. The girl on the tape was someone I had been dating. She had never acted before and she did a great job. That night, she insisted I make love to her as the rapist. A strange request, but it turned out to be some of the best sex I ever had. I'm glad she didn't call the cops for real.

To this day, no one has recognized me as the same player in all three scenes. If you watch the film again, you still may not be able to do so. Something weird and magical happened on that first FACES OF DEATH. We crossed the line from reality to unreality so many times that after a while the line was blurred forever.

CHAPTER 33: GRABBING THE HEADLINES

In the early eighties the public and the news media wanted to know about FACES OF DEATH. Everyone thought it was real. Even Dan Rather reported about our film on CBS NIGHTLY NEWS.

I kept a low profile. After all, I was seeking a legitimate film career and association with the brutality of FACES OF DEATH wasn't something I thought would be accepted in Disney-oriented Hollywood.

The more heat the film got the more people wanted to meet me and finally I gave in to the adulation. It hasn't stopped to this very day

The movie opened on 42nd Street in a sleazy theater. My brother went to the see the 12 noon sold-out show. A guy sitting behind my brother vomited during the monkey scene. People were screaming and some guys reluctantly ushered their girlfriends to the safety of the lobby. My brother called to tell me I had hit creative gold.

Our little movie spread like a virus and it is still blowing people away 35 years later!

Before the film was even sent out to theaters, I'll never forget the look on a friend's face when he watched a first cut. We were doing a color correction and my friend was the very the first person to see our movie. It was a look I have seen on many people's faces since then.

It was the look of a man who has peered into the beyond and, with a chill, realizes he has witnessed his own face of death.

CHAPTER 34: ON DEATH AND DYING

This movie still affects my life. As I grow older I realize I am far from immortal. In fact, I am in the last act of my life. I don't know where I'm headed but a Sikh once told me that when we die our spirit travels down a long white tunnel. As we zoom toward a white light at the end of the tunnel people from our past reach out to us.

The Sikh said it is crucial not take anyone's hand. Go straight for the light, he intoned, for it is in the light that you will find eternal peace.

I have a different theory. If you've ever stared at the night sky filled with an infinite amount of stars, I often think that when we die we become another star in the universe. My friends have different ideas about death based on their faith. One friend wants us to smoke his ashes in a joint, for in that act he believes he will achieve immortality.

In the end what does it mean? One thing is for sure: thanks to death we're all going on the ride of a lifetime with no seatbelts necessary. The bottom line is that we came in alone and we leave alone.

When I think about the light that the Sikh described or a star in the Universe that will soon be my resting place, I can't help but smile. Soon I will be home.